ERUPTION OF MOUNT VESUVIUS

A Brief Overview from Beginning to the End

HISTORY ENCOUNTERS

HISTORY ENCOUNTERS

Eruption of Mount Vesuvius

A Brief Overview from Beginning to the End

Contents

Mount Vesuvius, on the gulf of Naples in Italy, erupted in 79 AD killing many of the citizens of the town of Pompeii and surrounding towns and burying them under lava and debris.

One thousand, seven hundred years later, archeologists uncovered the perfectly preserved town under the lava layer. This has become one of the greatest archaeological finds, which has since become a massive tourist attraction. The Mountain has erupted many times since, and scientists remain on the alert for its next explosion.

Chapter One: Introduction

The famous Italian city of Pompeii was a Roman city from the city of Campania. This is in Italy, 23 kilometers south of Naples at the base of Mount Vesuvius. It has been preserved in the rock after a massive eruption on 24 August 79 AD. The eruption of Mount Vesuvius covered the whole city with volcanic fallout. The following day, blistering hot steam and gasses covered the area in clouds. Buildings crumpled, and the people were suffocated and crushed. The whole city was buried under a mountain of pumice and ash.

Scientists think that the cloud of hot gas and scalding ash would have killed the entire population within fifteen minutes. The estimated 2000 people who were killed were not killed by the molten lava, although they were engulfed in it. They were suffocated by a cloud of gas and ash which engulfed their lungs.

Studies by geologists and geographers have indicated that

the "pyroclastic flow," which is a thick quick flowing river of solidifying lava and hot ash, would have been accompanied by a cloud of lethal gas which, with a temperature of over 300 degrees celsius, was made up of CO2, particles of burning ash and volcanic glass. Some people would have died under a hail of lapilli, little volcanic stones, but most would have asphyxiated. Death might not have been instant, depending on where they were, and would have been terrible as the air in their lungs was replaced by this toxic cloud.

Scientists have described these "pyroclastic flows" as devastating. When the eruptive column collapses, volcanic ash rushes down the volcano slopes at incredible speeds of up to hundreds of kilometers per hour. The study of the eruption at Vesuvius and the resulting disaster helps scientists understand and trace pyroclastic currents. It's important to understand Mount Vesuvius for civil protection today.

The ruins of Pompeii are the most visited archeological area after the Colosseum. More than a million tourists a year visit this fascinating site. It's a not to be missed opportunity for any visitors to Italy.

Tourists are greeted by fascinating Greco-Roman buildings and many interesting artifacts revealing a sophisticated culture wiped out in an instant. There were amazing buildings like an elegant forum and a grand amphitheater. There were luxurious villas for the wealthy and different types of homes to suit all echelons of society. Some of these were already ancient, dating back to the fourth century BC. The remains of people sheltering from the eruption were perfectly preserved. Bakeries were even found with loaves still in the ovens. Society was preserved in a single moment in time, revealing an unchanged and undeveloped ancient city that has been a source of endless fascination to historians, biographers, and tourists alike.

We'll take this opportunity to examine the lost world of Pompeii and the ominous Mount Vesuvius, which still broods over it today. We'll look at society, archeology, and the roles of tourism, movies, and myths in keeping history alive.

Chapter Two: Mount Vesuvius

Pompeii in Art and Pop Culture: *So many books have been written on Pompeii and Vesuvius. These include academic tomes which examine geology, geography, and history and dramatic fiction pieces which create fictional characters who grip the reader as they live through the terror of the eruption of Vesuvius. There have been a number of interesting documentaries and dramatizations of life in Pompeii and the eruption of Vesuvius. Some are stylized fictional pieces, and others include serious examination of the science behind the eruption of Vesuvius.*

Mount Vesuvius was considered by the Greeks and Romans as being a sacred shrine to the demigod and mythical hero Heracles/Hercules. The little town of Herculaneum, which was built at its base and destroyed in the terrible eruption of AD 79, was named after him. The naming of the Mountain has caused some semantic discussion as it could also have been named after Zeus, who was called the god of rains and dew, Ves. Thus Hercules could be called the son of Ves, Vesuvius. In other sources, Vesuvius is named after words for smoke and hearth.

Let's start with describing the infamous Mount Vesuvius, which still broods over Pompeii today.

The Mountain at Peace

Mount Vesuvius is a Somma Stratovolcano which is a volcano that has been partly filled with a new central cone. It's located in the Campania area of Italy, approximately nine kilometers from Naples. It's close to the shore of the Gulf of Naples and is part of the Campanian volcanic arc.

If you look down on Vesuvius, you will see it consists of a large central cone that is encircled, partly at least, by the summit caldera. A caldera is a hollow, shaped like a cauldron from which the magma has erupted. This was caused by an earlier collapse of the mountain when it was much higher. It has an elevation of 1281 meters. Vesuvius is made up of two volcanos, Vesuvius is the one peak, and Monte Somma is the other. Vesuvius grew out of Monte Somma. The height of Vesuvius changes with every major eruption. The area between Mount Somma Ridge and the Vesuvius cone is called Giants Valley (Valle del Gigante). The peak of the cone holds a large crater that is approximately 600 meters across and 300 meters deep.

Vesuvius is an extremely well-known volcano and very volatile. In fact, it could be overdue for another eruption.

It seems crazy for people to live so close to Vesuvius, but the reason for it is simple. The land in the shadow of Vesuvius is incredibly fertile and arable. The lava and ash have deposited huge amounts of minerals, including nitrogen, phosphorus, and potassium, and these make for wonderful soil, particularly good for vineyards.

The hardened lava is very porous, soaking up rainfall much as a sponge would, lowering the need for irrigation, especially in the vineyard, as the vines can drink up the water, which is slowly released from the spongy rock.

The Wrath of Vesuvius

Before AD 79, when Vesuvius erupted, no name existed for the word Volcano. After the terrible eruption, the Mount was called a volcano after the Roman God Vulcan, the god of flame and metal forging.

When Vesuvius erupted in AD 79, it destroyed not only Pompeii.

Herculaneum, Stabiae, and Oplontis were also destroyed. The eruption threw clouds of ash, stones, and volcanic gasses 33 km into the air. Volcanic eruptions are a fascinating local phenomenon. The heat moves beneath the surface of the earth and is carried from the interior of the planet to the surface by the process of convection. The transfer of heat happens because of the movement of heated liquid, in this case, magma or molten rock. As the magma rises, it tears the earth's crust through gaps on its surface called volcanoes.

Between one and two thousand people died, although no one can be sure of the exact number. The only remaining eyewitness account is through a couple of letters from Pliny the Younger to Tacitus, the historian.

Vesuvius has erupted many times. It's also the last mainland European volcano to have erupted within the last century. It's classified as extremely dangerous because it has a population of 600 000 in its danger zone.

Vesuvius is not as old as volcanoes go, probably less than 200 000 years ago. It was largely dormant for centuries, except for an eruption thousands of years earlier, before it erupted and swallowed Pompeii and its neighboring towns. After that, however, it was like a beast that awoke and erupted at regular intervals every hundred years or so until 1944, which leads experts to believe that it's about to erupt again. Only eight eruptions in the last 1700 years have caused catastrophic loss of life and damage. The eruption of 1631 killed at least 3000 people. One wonders what will happen when Vesuvius erupts again. We'll have a look later at that possibility and the measures in place to preempt loss of life.

Chapter Three: The History of Pompeii

The Ruins of Pompeii: *The famous Italian city of Pompeii was a Roman city from the city of Campania. This is in Italy, 23 kilometers south of Naples at the base of Mount Vesuvius. It has been preserved in the rock after a massive eruption on 24 August 79 AD. The eruption of Mount Vesuvius covered the whole city with volcanic fallout. The following day, blistering hot steam and gasses covered the area in clouds. Buildings crumpled, and the people were suffocated and crushed. The whole city was buried under a mountain of pumice and ash.*

Pompeii is a well-preserved historical Roman city in Campania, Italy, 23 km to the southeast of Naples. It is situated next to the southeast base of the active volcano Mount Vesuvius. At about noon on 24 August 79 AD, an enormous eruption from the simmering Mount Vesuvius rained volcanic detritus over the whole city of Pompeii. Blistering gas clouds followed this. Houses and other buildings were obliterated, and the people were crushed by falling buildings or volcanic rocks or covered by a thick layer of pumice and ash. Pompeii slumbered beneath its ash shroud for centuries, which had perfectly conserved the structural and human remains. When the remains were finally excavated in the 18th century, the world was amazed at finding an intricate Greco-Roman city that had been perfectly preserved for so many years.

Pompeii was originally built on a spur made from an ancient prehistoric lava flow just north of the Sarnus River mouth. It had between ten and twenty thousand inhabitants when it was destroyed.

It appears definite that Pompeii, Herculaneum, and other nearby villages were initially settled by the Oscan-speaking people who were descendants of Neolithic dwellers in the province of Campania. The Oscan language became defunct when Latin deliberately supplanted Oscan. It was totally extinct by the end of the 1st century. Contemporary understanding of Oscan is from some 250 existing papers and inscriptions, which were composed in various alphabets, including a colonial Latin alphabet, a Greek alphabet, and an original rustic alphabet. Comparisons of the three languages gave historians the only information they have about the Oscan language. Archaeological data suggests that the Oscan town of Pompeii, which was located in a strategic position near the Sarnus River mouth, was soon influenced by the cultured Greek people who were settled across the bay from them. This Greek influence was contested when the Etruscans arrived at Campania in the 7th century. The Etruscans of Southern Italy impacted the early development of Pompeii by building a strongly walled city on a hill at the Sarno River mouth. The Etruscans' impact on the people of Pompeii stayed strong until King Hieron 1 of Syracuse destroyed their sea power in a sea battle just off Cumae in 474 AD. An additional period of Greek sovereignty then followed. After the end of the 5th century, the aggressive Samnites conquered Campania, and Pompeii and the other towns became unwilling Samnite citizens. The Samnites did refortify the aging infrastructure and ramparts to protect the Pompeians against the destructive forces of Hannibal's army. The Pompeians benefited from the refugees from Hannibal's onslaught on other tribes, though, as their numbers swelled and they went through a period of growth and prosperity.

Pompeii was first referred to in history in 310 BC when a Roman fleet engaged in the Second Samnite War docked at Pompeii at the Sarnus port and made an ineffectual raid on Nuceria, the neighboring city of Nuceria. At the conclusion of the Samnite wars, Campania came to be part of the confederation of Rome, and the towns were forced to become "allies" of Rome. They were not supportive of Rome and resisted being Romanized until the Social War. Rome's unwilling "allies" fought against their oppressor during the Social War. Pompeii united with the Italians in their uprising against Rome during this war and was blockaded and besieged by General Lucius

Cornelius Sulla BC 89. After this war, Pompeii and all of Italy south of the River Po were granted Roman citizenship. As a punishment for their rebellion, a colony of Roman ex-soldiers was established in Pompeii under the command of Publius Sulla, the general's nephew. Latin replaced Oscan as the official tongue of the people, and the culture, architecture, and institutions became Romanized.

After the alliance with the Romans, the Pompeians experienced increased wealth and prosperity when the Romans unlocked new markets for their allies. Various public works programs were begun during this time. These included repairs to the great Temple of Jupiter. After the Social War, Pompeii relied heavily on Rome politically and administratively.

The period that followed was turbulent. There was a riot in the amphitheater at Pompeii in 59 AD. This occurred between the Pompeians and the Nucerians. This was followed by the terrible earthquake in 62 AD that caused tremendous destruction in Pompeii and Herculaneum. Unfortunately, they did not recognize it as a sign of the catastrophic things to follow. The two cities had not recouped their losses after this catastrophe when the ultimate destruction vanquished them 17 years after this when Vesuvius erupted.

Chapter Four: Uncovering Pompeii

The Sculptures and Art of Pompeii: *The area of art history was occurring at the same time as these excavations, and typically sites like Herculaneum and Pompeii were of tremendous interest to the German scholar Johann Joachim Winckelmann, the man who first used the phrase "history of art." His statements on this region's discoveries excited Europeans' fervor for classical antiquity, i.e., ancient Greece and Rome. Grand Tour tourists from Britain and other countries chose to visit Pompeii and Herculaneum in the late 1800s.*

When Mount Vesuvius erupted in 79 AD, it obliterated and mostly buried Pompeii and Herculaneum and additional hamlets in the South of Italy under rock and ash. The exploration of these areas in modern times is as interesting as the history of the cities and furnishes a glimpse into archeology and art history.

Was Pompeii untouched for centuries?

The dominant belief of the immediate outcome of Mt. Vesuvius' spectacular eruption is that Pompeii, Herculaneum, and other sites, including Oplontis and Stabiae, remained buried beneath the ash and cold volcanic lava for centuries, untouched and undisturbed by human intervention. Geological and archaeological data, however, reveals that rescue operations were undertaken shortly after Vesuvius erupted. For example, tunnels were dug into the House of the Menander. It was also noted that some portions of the cities stayed visible for a while. The Pompeii forum colonnade stayed uncovered. During the Middle Ages, Pompeii remained completely abandoned, although the local residents still called the area the settlement or "La Città". Perhaps they nurtured the memories of the thriving city that had once existed.

Evacuations begin

While scholars from the Renaissance were probably aware of Pompeii and its devastation through several eyewitness written sources, the initial "archaeologist" to explore the ruins was clearly not impressed with his findings. From 1594-1600, Domenico Fontana, a local architect working on modern buildings in the area, unintentionally uncovered some inscriptions, wall paintings, and architectural blocks while he was excavating a canal. He showed no real interest, and no follow-up was undertaken for almost 1500 years despite the widespread interest in ancient artifacts and basic archaeology.

The 1700s saw the initial large-scale archeological excavations in this area, encouraged by the appetite for collecting works of historical artifacts and art as much as by the curiosity of scientists about past events. Additional accidental findings in the early 1700s motivated the King of Spain, Naples, and Sicily, to organize a survey in the Herculaneum area.

The authorized excavation started in October 1738, supervised by Rocque Joaquin de Alcubierre. He was a military engineer who burrowed through the virtually petrified volcanic elements to discover the remains of Herculaneum 20 meters beneath the surface.

This hazardous work, with the constant threat of toxic gasses and collapsing tunnels, resulted in a wealth of wall paintings and life-size bronze and marble sculptures. Another fascinating discovery was papyrus scrolls from the "Villa of the Papyri."

Several of these recouped artifacts adorn the King's palace. Because the field of Archaeology was still undeveloped, it was often translated as "treasure-hunting" rather than thorough research and meticulous documentation of the findings.

In 1750, Karl Jakob Weber, a Swiss engineer, commandeered the Herculaneum excavation from de Alcubierre. He introduced more careful techniques to the excavation site.

Weber's method of documenting the places where artifacts were found by making comprehensive drawings of the architectural remains was a foundation stone for the crucial protocols of modern-day archaeology. De Alcubierre changed his focus to Pompeii at this stage. Among the first excavations at Pompeii were the amphitheater and a stone notation corroborating the name of the town. "REI PUBLICAE POMPEIANORUM"

With discoveries from both Herculaneum and Pompeii exponentially on the increase, King Charles established in 1755, a Royal Academy in Naples committed to mapping out the locations and publishing important discoveries.

The Art Historians

The area of art history was occurring at the same time as these excavations. Typically, sites like Herculaneum and Pompeii were of tremendous interest to the German scholar Johann Joachim Winckelmann, the man who first used the phrase "history of art." His statements on the discoveries from this region excited the fervor of Europeans for classical antiquity i.e., ancient Greece and Rome. Grand Tour tourists from Britain and other countries chose to visit Pompeii and Herculaneum in the late 1800s.

What's still to Uncover?

Archeologists still haven't excavated everything destroyed by Mount Vesuvius.

Only about two-thirds of Pompeii and less of neighboring Herculaneum have been uncovered. Much of the area as yet excavated may stay so for years to come to protect the remains of these ancient cities. Herculaneum is now concealed under Ercolano. Though parts of the town have been demolished to facilitate excavations, modern thinking leads us to believe that they are unlikely to be excavated soon. This is a pity in some ways because no one knows what wealth of artifacts or mysteries from the past could still be discovered.

The reason for this is obvious, though. The ruins of Pompeii remained in a remarkable state of conservation for more than 1,600 years until after their excavation. Human interference and normal weathering have caused damage. Archaeologists are worried about the forthcoming preservation of the area, especially as Pompeii is a member of the World Monuments Fund, an organization devoted to conserving historical architecture. It is calculated that the preservation of the area will cost $335 million. With a great deal of Pompeii and Herculaneum still hidden under the volcanic detritus, there will be remains of the cities for centuries to come. It's the already excavated artifacts that are at risk.

Chapter Five: Everyday Entertainment in Ancient Pompeii

The people of Pompeii were heavily Romanized by the time the great eruption occurred. Besides doing normal things like working at their crafts, making a living, and raising their families, they had particular Romanized behaviors.

Injudicious Violence

The people of Pompeii enjoyed two of the popular forms of Roman entertainment. They loved the daily bath ritual in the opulent bathhouses that the city provided. Still, they were particularly fond of their amphitheater, where they were extremely violent even by Roman standards and certainly by today's standards. In the massive amphitheater that pitted people against dangerous beasts and gladiators against gladiators. The general populace flocked to these spectacles.

People came from neighboring towns like Nuceria, too, and they enjoyed the rowdy aftermath of the occasion. A riot that broke out between Pompeian and Nucerian fans in 59AD caused the authorities to close the amphitheater for ten years. Inscriptions have been found which extol the good looks, strength, and power of the gladiators, many of whom were foreign slaves. The successful among them enjoyed a hero status, especially among the women.

The Dramatic Arts

Attending the theater was another, less violent kind of popular recreation. Pompeii's theater was ancient, constructed in the second 2 BC in Greek design, and then extended and modernized during the period of Emperor Augustus into a Roman theater. Satires, comedies, and unsophisticated but entertaining farces were acted there, as were mimed enactments of popular mythology. The theater of ancient Greece was also popular based on wall paintings depicting their favorite shows. There was also a small music hall next door. Definite signs of an affluent society!

Fashionable Pompeii

Pompeii was a center of business and travel, monopolizing the river trade from the Gulf of Naples. Its richer citizens were familiar with all the popular beauty and fashion trends from Rome. The common dress for women throughout the Empire was called a stole. This was a long dress with draped pleats wrapped around the body and secured with attractive brooches called fibulae. Because their clothes were all similar, the women went to town with unique hairstyles and makeup.

Roman women favored white faces with dark eyes and very red lips. They made white creams with lead, animal fat, and chalk. Mollusks and ochre made excellent lipstick, and soot was used to darken the eye area. They used cinnamon and balsam-scented water to wash in, and the wealthy bathed in asses milk. Perfumes were made of rose, lavender, orange, saffron, and cardamom-infused oils, and they could admire their startling appearances in polished bronze or silver "mirrors."

They were fond of making blonde wigs from the hair of Celtic slaves, or they dyed it with harsh chemicals. Hairnets of gold thread and bone hairpins held their hair in elaborate styles. These complex hair towers often required the assistance of a few slaves to hold in place until the hair was secure and the wealthy lady could sally out in style.

All the people of Pompeii, except the extremely poor, would have enjoyed their meals which were simple but made of delicious fresh ingredients, at the local taverns on occasion, while the wealthy would have attended opulent banquets with other wealthy families.

Chapter Six: The Devastating Eruption

The Volcano: *Mount Vesuvius on the gulf of Naples in Italy erupted in 79 AD killing many the citizens of the town of Pompeii and surrounding towns, and burying them under lava and debris. The Mountain has erupted many times since, and scientists remain on the alert for its next explosion.*

The volcano indicated that it was about to erupt in 79 AD by several signs.

The Earthquake

As Mount Vesuvius led up to the eruptions, a string of earthquakes preceded them. Unfortunately, the citizens of Pompeii and Herculaneum had never seen an earthquake and had no idea how to interpret the signs. In 62 AD, twelve years before Vesuvius erupted, an enormous earthquake destroyed many of the buildings in Pompeii and the surrounding towns. Fortunately for some citizens, this was an unexpected blessing since it forced many of them to flee the city and ultimately settle in villages further away from the mighty volcano.

The Giant Erupts

When Vesuvius started to erupt, it ejected huge quantities of volcanic detritus high into the air. This then fell to earth and covered the surrounding towns. One way of understanding how severe the fallout was is to think of it in terms of the mass of elephants. The debris would have had a mass equivalent of 250 000 elephants per second. There was no chance of surviving that!

The whole disaster was over in just 24 hours. At about noon on 24 August 79 AD, Mount Vesuvius started to erupt. The initial stage of the eruption caused an explosion that sent millions of pumice stones, many thousands of meters, into the sky. These rocks then fell like water upon the neighboring towns, burying them completely over 5 hours. As the stones continued to plummet down to earth, they became larger, and over that period, they caused houses and buildings, and other structures to crumble and collapse.

The next stage of the eruption happened about 18 hours after the first stage when a brutal pyroclastic flow of lava gushed from the volcano, covering both Pompeii and Herculaneum in a huge layer of smoldering detritus in a matter of a few minutes. Finally, the dust over the cities and towns settled after 24 hours of ruthless bombardment by the volcano.

It used to be thought that people were immediately incinerated, and only their skeletons were left intact. However, findings of bodies still with their facial expressions of horror intact have caused scientists to question the original assessments.

It's thought nowadays that people trapped in a volcanic explosion undoubtedly die quickly, either from exposure to extreme heat or from suffocation. Afterward, however, their bodies started to cook. As they cooked, their skin and muscles became swollen, forcing the moisture from the soft body tissue inward toward the skeleton, effectively baking the skeleton rather than burning it.

Many people are thought to have escaped from the city during the initial stages of the eruption. It is thought that up to 15000 people were living in the area, and there is only evidence of between one and two thousand bodies. A few eyewitness accounts were later recorded as evidence that certain families escaped and continued to thrive through subsequent generations. It's very hard to be certain, and one can only speculate on the lucky survivors and what separated them from the less fortunate.

Chapter Seven: Other Times Vesuvius Erupted

The Streets of Pompeii Uncovered: *When Mount Vesuvius erupted in 79 AD, it obliterated and mostly buried Pompeii and Herculaneum and additional hamlets in the South of Italy under rock and ash. The exploration of these areas in modern times is as interesting as the history of the cities and furnishes a glimpse into archeology and art history.*

There have been many Vesuvius eruptions over the centuries. The most significant was, of course, the eruption of 79 AD.

Mt. Vesuvius is found on the southern border of an active volcanic area called the Phlegraean Fields. It is positioned along a subduction area where the Adriatic Microplate is buried under the Tyrrhenian Sea, the Western Mediterranean. Mt. Vesuvius is perched on ancient sedimentary rocks, including Jurassic limestone, Triassic dolomite Jurassic limestones, and Tertiary sandstone. It's also situated on youngish volcanic rocks called gray Campanian Tuffs.

Mt. Vesuvius undoubtedly has the lengthiest historical documented volcanic eruptions in recorded history. The now well-known eruption of 79 A.D. was documented by Pliny the Younger in two messages to his friend, Tacitus, a Roman historian. His uncle Pliny the Elder, died in an endeavor to save friends from the catastrophe.

A.D. 79

This eruption which eradicated Pompeii, was preceded by an enormous earthquake in 62 AD, and restorations were still being undertaken when Vesuvius erupted. Seneca suggested that the earthquake was a precursor to the eruption as it indicated increasing magmatic pressure. 600 sheep suffered carbon dioxide poisoning, which also indicated trouble brewing.

The volcanic eruption has been described in Section 5, but a few further facts are of interest.

- The people on the West side of Vesuvius were unharmed.
- Many people managed to flee the town.
- People in Herculaneum escaped by boat, but those caught on the shore were instantly killed.
- In the Southern towns, like Pompeii, the pyroclastic flow with the heat of over 500 C vaporized all organic material, including human flesh.

1631

The eruption of 1631 was considered a Sub-Plinian eruption, meaning it was not as severe as the Pompeian one. Vesuvius had been dormant for over 130 years, and there were tell-tale signs of an eruption. There were two earthquakes that year and the wells dried up in December. The cattle and other livestock were restless the night before the mountain erupted. On 16 December, a series of explosions occurred, and an ash cloud full of lightning emerged from the top of the mountain. Fissures appeared on the sides and base, and toxic fumes and lava rolled down the west side. At least 40 000 people fled in terror to Naples early in the morning after a night of earthquakes. The summit exploded, and lava poured out and destroyed towns to the west. It reached the sea, and another earthquake caused a sequence of tsunamis. Several towns were destroyed. At least 4000 people died.

1779 to 1906

- In 1779, a lava fountain 4 km high erupted.
- In 1794, an eruption caused lava to flow to the sea, destroying the town of Torre del Greco and causing 18 deaths.
- In 1906, a lava torrent 3 km high cascaded down towards Boscotrecase and Ottaviani, killing 218 people.

1944

This was the date of the last significant eruption.

- On 1 March, the observatory monitored tremors and small earthquakes. The lava level decreased, and several explosions partially caused the central crater to collapse.
- On 17 March, seismic activity ceased
- On 18 March, it rose sharply, and the crater opened. Explosions caused lava to flow down the slopes for several days.
- On 19 March, lava destroyed St Sebastiano and Massa.
- On 20 March, the lava fountain was at least 2 km high.
- Between the 21 and 26 March, the mountain settled down, producing white ash as its fury died. Twenty-eight people lost their lives.

Vesuvius entered another period of repose, leaving us with the question. When will the Mountain erupt again?

Chapter Eight: When will Vesuvius Erupt again?

Forever Preserved in Lava: *It is thought that up to 15000 people were living in the area, and there is only evidence of between one and two thousand bodies. A few eyewitness accounts were later recorded as evidence that certain families escaped and continued to thrive through subsequent generations. It's very hard to be certain, and one can only speculate on the lucky survivors and what separated them from the less fortunate.*

Vesuvius had its last severe eruption in 1944. Fortunately, a new study by volcano experts suggests that it could be a couple of hundred years before it explodes again.

Vesuvius is undoubtedly Europe's most hazardous volcano. Three million people reside in its immediate proximity, and as history has shown, the mountain has been dire in terms of the destruction of life and property.

So, the question is: When will Vesuvius blow again, and how powerful might the eruption be?

A Zurich research group, in collaboration with Italian researchers, has looked closely at the four vastest eruptions over a period of 10,000 years to assess whether such a hazardous event might be anticipated in the near future.

The four eruptions studied include the Avellino eruption of 3,950 years ago and the eruption of AD 79 that devastated the Roman towns of Pompeii and Herculaneum.

The study examined the age of garnet crystals which are present in volcanic rock. The garnets grow in the magma, which is stored in the magma chamber. This chamber is in the upper crust within Vesuvius. Knowing the age of the crystals makes it possible to work out how long the magma resided in the chamber before the volcanic eruption.

Usually, researchers use zircon to make this assessment, but Vesuvius magma is too alkaline to support zircons, and it's perfect for growing garnets. To deduce the age of the garnets, the researchers use radioactive uranium and thorium to calculate with the isotope ratio the crystallization age of the mineral. By utilizing the crystallization age of the garnets, the researchers are able to show that the largely volatile magma type, the so "phonolitic" magma, is stored in a lava pool in the upper crust of the volcano for some thousands of years before the inflow of more basic, and much hotter, magma from the low crust activates an eruption.

For the two ancient events, the researchers inferred that the phonolitic magma occupied the chamber for approximately 5,000 years. It was stocked in this pool for approximately 1,000 years for later eruptions.

It appears likely to these researchers that, although Vesuvius has had a reservoir of magma existing under it for at least 10 000 years, it takes time for the "magic" hotter lava to build up enough beneath the phonolitic magma to cause a serious eruption. Still, there is no question that Vesuvius has the potential to create a very nasty explosion. It seems unlikely that the short period since 1944 would give it the oomph it needs to create a real monster of an eruption, but it's not impossible.

To avoid such a nasty eventuality, however, Vesuvius and its scary big brother, the Phlegraean Fields, are constantly monitored by Italy's National Institute of Geophysics and Volcanology. An emergency plan is also in place to ensure that the Naples area can be fully evacuated in case the Mountain decides to throw a curveball.

Chapter Nine: Pompeii for Tourists

Touring Pompeii Today: *Visiting Pompeii is an excellent plan if you're visiting Italy. It is a fascinating experience and can be quite challenging if you decide to climb Vesuvius. Pompeii is open from Monday to Sunday, from 9 to 5 pm in Winter and from 9 to 7 pm in Summer. The last entry is at 3.30. in Winter and 5.30 in Summer. Pompeii is closed on Christmas and New Year's day.*

Visiting Pompeii is an excellent plan if you're visiting Italy. It is a fascinating experience and can be quite challenging if you decide to climb Vesuvius.

Pompeii is open from Monday to Sunday, from 9 to 5 pm in Winter and from 9 to 7 pm in Summer. The last entry is at 3.30. in Winter and 5.30 in Summer. Pompeii is closed on Christmas and New Year's day

Tickets can be bought online or on-site. It's free to visit Pompeii on the first Sunday of the month, but it is usually extremely busy.

Visiting Pompeii

Toilet facilities and water are available on site. There is a cafeteria available for fast food.

The easiest way to arrive at Pompeii is by the regional train called the Circumvesuviana. The train is often very busy and has a reputation for pickpockets, so care should be taken. Taxis and other train and bus services do exist.

Tourists will not be allowed to take a bag into the ruins. This is for security purposes but also because bags rub against the walls and damage their fragile surfaces. It's also really tiring to carry a large bag with one in the tight squeeze of the ruins, particularly the brothel house or the Lupanar with its beautiful wall paintings.

It's a good idea to take a water bottle as there are faucets all along the way, and it gets really hot so staying hydrated is extremely important. Many faucets are set above Roman drinking troughs, which gives them quite an authentic feel.

The Casa del Menandro, also called the House of Menander, was a grand villa in Pompeii. Excavated and restored in the 1920s, it's a wonderful building to visit. Food, drink, and famous gelatos are available for sale near this fascinating site. It's also a good idea to bring snacks from home as the cafeterias can be crowded.

It's not a good idea to take the unofficial guided tours because while they are quite a bit cheaper than the guided tours, they are usually very crowded and hard to understand. The tickets for gate entry are 16€, but tourists should be careful not to be conned by fake ticket booths outside the gate. Buying tickets online is a good idea because ticket numbers are capped if it gets too busy. There is also talk of restrictions on numbers in the future to preserve the ruins from further harm.

Official Guided Tours

The official guided tour is very helpful. The ruins are vast and poorly signposted, and it's easy to get confused or lost. The official tour is good value for money with small groups and an experienced guide for only €15. It's nearly impossible to see enough of Pompeii in a half day though. Even a full day is a push because the main sites are far apart, and the ruins are huge. So tourists should make time to enjoy them. Both the large Amphitheater and the Garden of Fugitives are must-sees, but they are far apart. It's essential to get a map to make sure that one takes in all the important sites. And that one wears good shoes and sunscreen. The city is very hot, and the sun bakes down, especially if one wants to climb Vesuvius. Fortunately, tourists can get a bus trip up the mountain if they're not inclined to walk. Either way, they should prepare for a long, hot, fascinating experience that should not be missed.

Chapter Ten: Pompeii through Film and Media

So many books have been written on Pompeii and Vesuvius. These include academic tomes which examine geology, geography, and history and dramatic fiction pieces which create fictional characters who grip the reader as they live through the terror of the eruption of Vesuvius. There have been a number of interesting documentaries and dramatizations of life in Pompeii and the eruption of Vesuvius. Some are stylized fictional pieces, and others include serious examination of the science behind the eruption of Vesuvius. There has also been a particularly bad movie released in 2014, which Rotten Tomatoes and other critics hated, but the general public seemed to enjoy.

We'll take a brief look at an example of each of these types of media representations.

Pompeii the Movie

Pompeii the Movie is a gladiator's tale set in the final days of the Roman city before the eruption of Vesuvius. It's extremely violent and full of carnage. Gladiators battle to the death, soldiers slaughter villagers, prisoners beat each other up over minor affronts, and several scenes conclude with corpses piling up.

The film was released in February 2014 and had a great cast, but it is filled with ridiculous scenes, unrealistic action and impossible stunts, wooden language, and a disappointing conclusion. Although no doubt not everybody would agree with that opinion.

Pompeii: The Last Day

In this 2003 dramatized documentary, the story of the eruption of Mount Vesuvius in 79 AD is told. This explosion buried the Roman cities of Pompeii and Herculaneum in pumice and ash, destroying all those people trapped in the terrible gap between the volcano and the sea. The documentary depicts the various stages of the eruption. It's an interesting, factual account of the disaster written by Edward Canfor-Dumas.

The Fires of Vesuvius

Although Pompeii still fails to give up its mysteries, Mary Beard writes a fascinating account of what preceded the disaster. From politics to sex, religion to food, literacy to slavery, she gives a big picture of what life might have been like for the citizens of the lost town.

Vesuvius eradicated Pompeii in 79 CE, and its ruins give us the most credible information about what life was like in the Roman Empire. But the explosions are a small part of the tale. In The Fires of Vesuvius, published in 2010, lauded historian Mary Beard gives us a graphic understanding of what life was really like before the Mountain buried Pompeii forever.

Pompeii: The Tragic Eruption of Mount Vesuvius (A History of the City and the Eruption of Mount Vesuvius)

Crystel Corkery writes a fascinating archeological description of the resurrection of Pompeii, including plans for the modern restoration of the city.

- In its pages, you will also discover fascinating findings disclosed by archaeological digs
- The political lives, wars, and cultures that shaped the vivid, diverse culture of Pompeii
- Personal tales of the Pompeiian people that have endured

to this day
- How Pompeii evolved to be one of the wealthiest societies in the Roman Empire

Published in 2022, the book is topical, relevant and up-to-date on everything you want to know about Pompeii. And there's no shortage of other literature about Pompeii.

Discussion Questions 1

The people of Pompeii were highly Romanized. How did this happen? What did it mean to them as far as lifestyle was concerned?

Discussion Questions 2

Why were and still are the slopes of Vesuvius good for agriculture? Does this explain why people live in a risk area? What do you think?

Discussion Questions 3

The volcano caused terrible devastation. Explain what happened to the people caught in the eruption. Was it a quick way to go?

Discussion Questions 4

How were Pompeii and Herculaneum affected differently? Why was this? Explain the circumstances.

Discussion Questions 5

What can tourists see in Pompeii? What advice would you give to a potential tourist? Would you like to visit Pompeii?

Discussion Questions 6

Will Pompeii erupt again? And if so, when? What do the experts say?

Discussion Questions 7

Describe the other times Vesuvius erupted. Which was the most severe? What do you think?

Discussion Questions 8

People take risks around places prone to natural disasters. Do you agree? Why is this?

True or False Questions

1. **True or False.** Pompeii, the Movie, was particularly bad. Rotten Tomatoes and other critics hated it. It was a poor rendition of a terrible event.

2. **True or False.** Scientists are using zircons to read the age of the Magma in Vesuvius. This will help them decide when Vesuvius will erupt again. It's a clever concept.

3. **True or False.** In 1631 Vesuvius erupted. This was called a sub-Plinian eruption. This means it was not as severe as the Pompeian one.

4. **True or False.** The Pompeians were very violent. They loved watching gladiators killing each other. They hated any form of culture.

5. **True or False.** Only about two-thirds of Pompeii and less of neighboring Herculaneum have been uncovered. Much of the areas as yet excavated may stay so for years to come to protect the remains of these ancient cities.

6. **True or False.** Vesuvius and the Phlegraean Fields are

constantly monitored to avoid another nasty eruption. Italy's National Institute of Geophysics and Volcanology closely monitors the situation. There is also an emergency plan in place.

7. ***True or False.*** Tourists cannot take big bags into Pompeii. This is because they steal artifacts. It's a big problem.

8. ***True or False.*** The people of Pompeii originally came from Rome. It was a Roman colony. No other nation ever lived in Pompeii.

True or False Answer

1. True

2. False. They are using garnets to read the Magma. Zircons cannot grow in Vesuvius. The environment is too alkaline.

3. True

4. False. The people of Pompeii also liked the arts. They loved the theater. They even had a music hall.

5. True.

6. True.

7. False. The bags of tourists rub on the walls. This damages the delicate artwork. This is very frustrating for the curators.

8. False. The Oscan-speaking people were the original citizens of Pompeii. The Greeks followed them. The Romans came later.

Conclusion

The Power of Nature

While the whole disaster of Mount Vesuvius' dramatic eruption was over in just one day, it was a day like no other. It served to remind us of the terrifying power of nature.

At approximately noon on 24 August 79 AD, Mount Vesuvius began its massive eruption. The early stage of the eruption created an explosion that rocketed millions of tons of pumice stones thousands of meters into the sky. These rocks then tumbled like water cascading down a waterfall in a torrent of fiery stone upon Pompeii and the neighboring towns, totally burying them over a half-day period. As the stones plummeted down to earth, they grew in size and caused the famous Roman buildings and people's homes to collapse under their weight.

Then the devastating pyroclastic flow of lava gushed in an ominous red stream from the volcano, covering Pompeii in a massive layer of burning volcanic debris in a matter of a few minutes. While those in neighboring Herculaneum who failed to escape by sea were incinerated on the beach, and the town was buried in a massive mudslide.

The settlements on the other side of Mount Vesuvius escaped unscathed. This brings to mind a question about natural disasters. Is it a case of being caught out at the wrong time?

Earthquakes, volcanos, tsunamis, tornadoes, etc. Mankind is helpless in the face of the mighty power of nature unleashed, but there's no question that it's usually more than a question of bad luck.

In the case of Vesuvius in 79 AD, more than ten years before, the Mountain started to awaken and show its power through a mighty earthquake. The people could have been alerted if they had been responsive. Domestic animals showed signs of being restive and unsettled a day before the mountain erupted. Possibly if the people had been observant, they would have noticed that wild birds and animals had fled the area as they did during the Tsunami in Thailand and Indonesia in the late 1900s. And then, of course, people choose to live in an area that is prone to being a natural disaster zone. The Pompeians chose to live on the fertile mountain slopes of Vesuvius as they do today. The porous rock holds water and slowly releases it into their vineyards, and the soil is rich with minerals that feed their crops. They weigh up risk against return, and sometimes the Mountain wins.

Fortunately, today modern monitoring equipment ensures that the Mountain is carefully observed at all times. There will be no surprises, and people will almost certainly be able to evacuate the area in time. However, even so, the next time Vesuvius erupts, there could still be a devastating loss of property and livelihood. With human nature being what it is, however, they'll be back in the shadow of the mountain in no time, rebuilding their lives and knowing that they have the window of many generations of peaceful coexistence with the mighty volcano.

Bibliography (Works Cited)

1. 11 Amazing Facts about Mount Vesuvius. (Staff Writer). Pompeii Tours (Date not listed) https://www.pompeiitou rs.it/blog/11-amazing-facts-about-mount-vesuvius/

2. Is Vesuvius Taking an Extended Siesta? (ETH Zurich). Science Daily, (January 20, 2022) https://www.scienceda ily.com/releases/2022/01/220120125422.htm

3. Pompeii, (Wilhelmina Feemster Jashemski) Britannica, (Updated 5 January 2023). https://www.britannica.com/ place/Pompeii

4. The rediscovery of Pompeii and the other cities of Vesuvius, (Dr. Francesca Tronchin). Khan Academy, (updated December 2022). https://www.khanacademy.org/hum anities/ancient-art-civilizations/roman/x7e914f5b:pom peii/a/the-rediscovery-of-pompeii-and-the-other-cities -of-vesuvius

5. Mount Vesuvius Didn't Kill Everyone in Pompeii. Where Did the Survivors Go?, (Laura Geggel). Live Science, (3

May 2021) https://www.livescience.com/64854-where-pompeii-refugees-fled.html

6. https://theromanguy.com/italy-travel-blog/pompeii/can-it-erupt-again-mount-vesuvius-facts-and-history/

7. What if Mount Vesuvius Erupted Today? (Staff Writer). CBC, (October 2022). CBC.https://www.cbc.ca/natureofthings/features/what-if-mount-vesuvius-erupted-today

Images (License-Free)

The Volcano: Mount Vesuvius on the gulf of Naples in Italy erupted in 79 AD killing many the citizens of the town of Pompeii and surrounding towns, and burying them under lava and debris. The Mountain has erupted many times since, and scientists remain on the alert for its next

explosion. **https://pixabay.com/photos/vesuvius-volcano-destinations-italy-4468901/**

The Ruins of Pompeii: The famous Italian city of Pompeii was a Roman city from the city of Campania. This is in Italy, 23 kilometers south of Naples at the base of Mount Vesuvius. It has been preserved in the rock after a massive eruption on 24 August 79 AD. The eruption of Mount Vesuvius covered the whole city with volcanic fallout. The following day, blistering hot steam and gasses covered the area in clouds. Buildings crumpled, and the people were suffocated and crushed. The whole city was buried under a mountain of pumice and ash. **https://commons.wikimedia.org/wiki/File:Ruins_of_Pompeii_with_the_Vesuvius.jpg**

The Streets of Pompeii Uncovered: When Mount Vesuvius erupted in 79 AD, it obliterated and mostly buried Pompeii and Herculaneum and additional hamlets in the South of Italy under rock and ash. The exploration of these areas in modern times is as interesting as the history of the cities and furnishes a glimpse into archeology and art history. **https://pixabay.co m/photos/pompeii-italy-roman-ancient-travel-2375135/**

Forever Preserved in Lava: It is thought that up to 15000 people were living in the area, and there is only evidence of between one and two thousand bodies. A few eyewitness accounts were later recorded as evidence that certain families escaped and continued to thrive through subsequent generations. It's very hard to be certain, and one can only speculate on the lucky survivors and what separated them from the less fortunate. **https://pixabay.com/photos/pompeii-italy-man-statue-stonework-253364/**

The Sculptures and Art of Pompeii: The area of art history was occurring at the same time as these excavations, and typically sites like Herculaneum and Pompeii were of tremendous interest to the German scholar Johann Joachim Winckelmann, the man who first used the phrase "history of art." His statements on this region's discoveries excited Europeans' fervor for classical antiquity, i.e., ancient Greece and Rome. Grand Tour tourists from Britain and other countries chose to visit Pompeii and Herculaneum in the late 1800s. **https://pixabay.com/photos/pompeii-italy-naples-ancient-2580010/**

Pompeii in Art and Pop Culture: So many books have been written on Pompeii and Vesuvius. These include academic tomes which examine geology, geography, and history and dramatic fiction pieces which create fictional characters who grip the reader as they live through the terror of the eruption of Vesuvius. There have been a number of interesting documentaries and dramatizations of life in Pompeii and the eruption of Vesuvius. Some are stylized fictional pieces, and others include serious examination of the science behind the eruption of Vesuvius. **https://pixabay.com/photos/pompei i-vesuvies-roman-monument-2760337/**

Touring Pompeii Today: Visiting Pompeii is an excellent plan if you're visiting Italy. It is a fascinating experience and can be quite challenging if you decide to climb Vesuvius. Pompeii is open from Monday to Sunday, from 9 to 5 pm in Winter and from 9 to 7 pm in Summer. The last entry is at 3.30. in Winter and 5.30 in Summer. Pompeii is closed on Christmas and New Year's day. **https://pixabay.com/photos/pompeii-town-sq uare-vezuv-1233933/**

References (Works Cited)

1. 11 Amazing Facts about Mount Vesuvius. (Staff Writer). Pompeii Tours (Date not listed) https://www.pompeiitours.it/blog/11-amazing-facts-about-mount-vesuvius/

2. Is Vesuvius Taking an Extended Siesta? (ETH Zurich). Science Daily, (January 20, 2022) https://www.sciencedaily.com/releases/2022/01/220120125422.htm

3. Pompeii, (Wilhelmina Feemster Jashemski) Britannica, (Updated 5 January 2023). https://www.britannica.com/place/Pompeii

4. The rediscovery of Pompeii and the other cities of Vesuvius, (Dr. Francesca Tronchin). Khan Academy, (updated December 2022). https://www.khanacademy.org/humanities/ancient-art-civilizations/roman/x7e914f5b:pompeii/a/the-rediscovery-of-pompeii-and-the-other-cities-of-vesuvius

5. Mount Vesuvius Didn't Kill Everyone in Pompeii. Where Did the Survivors Go?, (Laura Geggel). Live Science, (3 May 2021) https://www.livescience.com/64854-where-pompeii-refugees-fled.html

6. https://theromanguy.com/italy-travel-blog/pompeii/can-it-erupt-again-mount-vesuvius-facts-and-history/

7. What if Mount Vesuvius Erupted Today? (Staff Writer). CBC, (October 2022). CBC.https://www.cbc.ca/natureofthings/features/what-if-mount-vesuvius-erupted-today

www.ingramcontent.com/pod-product-compliance
Lightning Source LLC
Chambersburg PA
CBHW061258140726
47998CB00006B/2262